A DAY WITH THE
ARTIST

Nia Gould

Written and
edited by
Jocelyn Norbury

Illustrated by
Nia Gould

Designed by Barbara Ward
Cover design by John Bigwood

First published in Great Britain in 2025 by
LOM ART, an imprint of Michael O'Mara Books Limited,
9 Lion Yard, Tremadoc Road, London SW4 7NQ

 www.mombooks.com/lom

 Michael O'Mara Books

 @OMaraBooks

 @lomart.books

A CIP catalogue record for this book is available from the British Library.

ISBN: 978-1-915751-30-0

10 9 8 7 6 5 4 3 2 1

This book was printed in December 2024 by Shenzhen Wing King Tong
Paper Products Co. Ltd., Shenzhen, Guangdong, China.

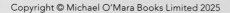

Step into the Studio

Have you ever wondered where artists create their amazing paintings, sculptures and drawings? Join this behind-the-scenes tour to discover how different artists worked, learn about the spaces and places that have inspired them and get to know their best works of art.

In these pages you will meet nine world-famous artists and read about their fascinating lives, then explore the places where they have worked. Each studio scene is packed with information to help you understand their colourful and creative worlds.

There are lots of things to spot, including six cheeky mice hiding in each scene. Find the answers at the back of the book along with a handy art movement cheat sheet, as well as a fun quiz to test your knowledge.

What are you waiting for?
Turn the page to start the tour ...

Leonardo da Vinci

Artist, scientist, inventor – Leonardo must be one of the cleverest people who ever lived!

Leonardo was an Italian artist who was brilliant at maths, writing, music and engineering as well as painting, drawing and sculpture.

Even though he was a genius, Leonardo never actually went to school. Instead, he was taught to read and write at home, and then studied with another artist, Andrea del Verrocchio.

In his lifetime he was mainly famous for his paintings, making portraits for very rich noblemen. He lived in a house given to him by the King of France!

Many of his paintings took a long time to complete. *The Last Supper*, one of the world's greatest masterpieces, took him over three years.

These objects tell us important information about Leonardo. Can you spot them in his studio on the next page?

Leonardo is probably most famous for his painting of a woman called **Mona Lisa**. Her mysterious smile has captured imaginations for centuries.

He was often thinking up new **inventions**. Most, like this flying machine, were never made, but some people think they were early ideas for things like the helicopter and the telephone.

A huge animal lover, Leonardo studied how **birds** fly, but also bought caged birds just to set them free.

A keen amateur **musician**, multi-talented Leonardo loved making up poems and putting them to music.

Things to spot

A blue **jar**

A red **notebook**

Five curious **pigeons**

Six **mice** watching Leonardo at work

A **flute**

Claude Monet

One of the greatest French artists of all time, Claude was a key figure of the 'Impressionist' art movement.

Claude showed an early talent for art when he began drawing funny cartoons of teachers at school. Luckily they were so good he never got into trouble!

As an Impressionist, he was interested in capturing the effect of changing light on colours, so he painted the same scene again and again, at different times of day.

The art movement Impressionism got its name from one of Claude's paintings, called *Impression: Sunrise*.

He loved to use oil paints and to paint 'en plein air', which means 'outdoors' in French. The Impressionists much preferred this to working inside a studio.

These pictures of Claude's garden can tell us a lot about him as an artist. Can you spot them on the next page?

Water lilies were one of his favourite things to paint. He captured them in all weathers over a 30-year period.

Most people would recognize this **bridge** from Claude's most famous painting. He had it built specially when he became famous and wealthy.

Using white paint, he experimented with capturing how **light** reflects on water.

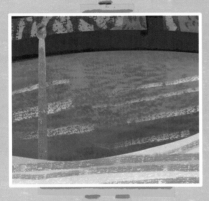

Claude often worked on **a few paintings** at the same time. If he wasn't happy with his work, he sometimes threw the canvases into the pond!

Things to spot

A bright green **frog**

A yellow paintbrush **pot**

Six colourful, camouflaged **mice**

A **painting** of a woman holding a **parasol**

A **bear** wearing a **pink** jumper

Vincent van Gogh

Vincent was an artist who loved nothing more than setting up his easel outdoors and painting.

Vincent was born in the Netherlands, but hopped over to a town called Arles, in the south of France, so he could enjoy the beautiful scenery.

He loved to paint local scenes with trees, flowers and the night sky. He did many portraits, some of himself and some of the people in Arles.

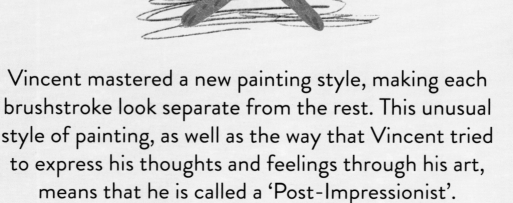

Vincent mastered a new painting style, making each brushstroke look separate from the rest. This unusual style of painting, as well as the way that Vincent tried to express his thoughts and feelings through his art, means that he is called a 'Post-Impressionist'.

Discover what inspired Vincent's paintings as you bounce around his town on the next page!

His most famous paintings are of the **sunflowers** that grew around Arles. He painted eight almost identical versions of this picture!

One of Vincent's best friends was another artist called **Paul Gauguin**. Vincent looked up to him and Paul helped him develop his own style of painting. Sadly they argued a lot.

Vincent's favourite colour combination was **blue** and **yellow**. He thought using them together made the colours look more vibrant. Do you agree?

This yellow house was where Vincent **lived** with **Paul Gauguin**.

Things to spot

A vase of **sunflowers**

A red **pencil**

A cat carrrying a **baguette**

A slice of **watermelon**

Six **mice** enjoying the sunny street

Henri Matisse

Henri used bright colours and unusual shapes to express himself, creating an exciting new art style.

Born in France in 1869, Henri trained as a lawyer before deciding to become an artist.

For a while, he mostly made paintings. He used lots of bright colours and painted without worrying whether the painting looked lifelike.

His new art style was so unusual that lots of people found it shocking. They labelled Henri and his artist friends 'fauves' which means 'wild beasts'.

When Henri got older, he struggled to stand up to paint. He started making collages from his wheelchair, or even his bed, by cutting shapes out of paper.

You can learn more about Henri by exploring his sunny studio and discovering his favourite things.

Lots of Henri's art was inspired by his love of jazz music that he listened to on something called a **phonograph**. He even named some of his collages *Jazz*.

Henri cut out lots of **leaf shapes** to make his colourful collages. They might look similar but each shape is different from the rest.

A lover of nature and animals, Henri included his pet **doves** and **cats** in lots of his artwork.

"There are always **flowers** for those who want to see them," Henri famously said. He loved to surround himself with brightly coloured plants.

Things to spot

Six cheeky **mice**

A pair of red **scissors**

A yellow **bird**

Two bright pink **plant pots**

A bobbing **sailboat**

Pablo Picasso

Pablo was brilliant at drawing, but is most famous for creating a new style of art called 'Cubism'.

Born in Spain in 1881, Pablo stood out as a great artist from an early age. He could draw almost anything, in any style.

He liked experimenting with new ways of representing what he saw. In his Blue Period he coloured everything using only shades of blue.

During his Cubist Period he tried to show the same thing from lots of different angles at once. His wonky faces show features from the side and the front.

He painted one of the most famous pictures in the world, *Guernica*, in protest about the Spanish Civil War.

Check out Pablo's studio on the next page to spot the things that inspired him.

Pablo's father kept **pigeons** and taught his son how to paint them. Birds feature in lots of Pablo's art and he even named his daughter Paloma, which is Spanish for dove!

Lump the dachshund was one of Pablo's favourite pets and appears in some of his paintings.

Pablo loved to wear his special **striped shirt**. You will almost always see him wearing it in pictures.

As well as painting pictures, Pablo made many **sculptures** in his lifetime, although these are less famous than his paintings.

Things to spot

A cute **pup** wearing a **green** collar

A **cat** sculpture

A **newspaper**

A pink **pencil**

Six **mice** enjoying the colourful studio

Salvador Dalí

Salvador's paintings and sculptures captured the weird and wonderful world of his imagination.

One of the main artists of the 'Surrealist' movement, Salvador made art that felt bizarre and dreamlike.

A self-proclaimed eccentric, he painted melting clocks and floating eyes. He also made sculptures of things like lobster-shaped telephones.

He tried to capture the world of his imagination, rather than making art that seemed lifelike.

As well as his more unusual work, Salvador is also famous for the art he made to protest against the Spanish Civil War in the 1930s.

Look closely at Salvador's garden on the next page and you might spot these unusual items.

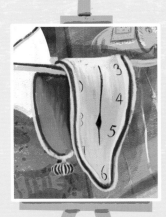

He loved to paint **melting clocks** in his art. We think this was his way of showing that time can be flexible.

At one time, it was thought that Salvador had a pet **anteater**! It turned out it was a stunt and he had just taken one out for a walk.

Salvador loved to stand out from the crowd with his funny **moustache**, long hair and unusual outfits.

This sofa in the shape of actress Mae West's **lips** has become an icon of the Surrealist art movement.

Things to spot

Seven hungry **ants**

A sunbathing **lobster**

A giant **egg**

Five fluttering **butterflies**

Six sneaky **mice**

Frida Kahlo

Famous for her colourful self-portraits, Frida is one of the most important Mexican artists in history.

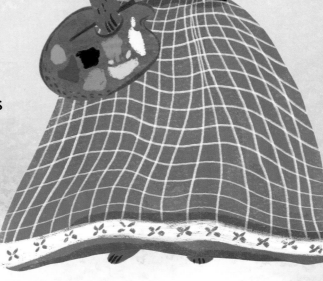

When Frida was five years old, she suffered a serious illness called polio but managed to recover.

At the age of 18, she was in an accident on a bus and was badly injured. While she was recovering in bed she began to paint.

She painted her feelings and emotions using traditional Mexican colours.

When Frida was older, she married a famous artist called Diego Rivera. They lived and painted together in Casa Azul, the 'Blue House', which was the house Frida grew up in.

Learn more about Frida's favourite things as you explore her colourful garden on the next page.

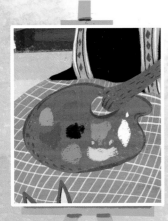

Frida was well known for wearing **bright colours**, flowers in her hair and jewellery.

She said that she painted **self-portraits** because "I am the person I know best."

She often exaggerated her own facial features in her paintings. Her self-portraits often show her with large **bushy eyebrows** and a moustache.

Frida had lots of **unusual pets** including a pair of spider monkeys, a fawn and a parrot called Bonito.

Things to spot

Six **mice** hiding in the garden

Two green and yellow **birds**

A ginger **cat**

A **cactus** with orange flowers

A Mexican **flag**

Andy Warhol

'Pop Art' relates to popular culture, which can be anything that is fashionable. Andy thought that by using objects that people recognized, he could make them see everyday things in a different way.

Andy lived in New York City, where he worked as an illustrator before making his name as an artist.

He didn't stick to one type of art but explored lots of different mediums, such as painting, screenprinting, photography, film and sculpture.

24 GIANT SIZE PKGS.
HOG WASH
HOG WASH
SHINES WASHING FAST

As a child, Andy developed a hand-printing technique where he traced an image with ink and then pressed it on to another piece of paper. This allowed him to repeat an image over and over again. This style of art would become his trademark.

Join Andy's party on the next page and see if you can spot some of his most inspirational objects!

One of his most famous pictures is a print of a **can of soup** – he said that he ate a can of soup every day for 20 years!

Cats were Andy's favourite animal. He lived with his mother and 25 feline friends, who were all called Sam.

Andy threw lots of parties at his studio, the **Factory**, in New York City. He had lots of famous friends and loved to be surrounded by creative people.

Andy predicted that "in the future, everyone will be world **famous** for 15 minutes."

Things to spot

A **party** invitation

Four **polaroid** pictures

A blue **pencil**

Six **mice** partying at the Factory

A **cat** wearing a name badge

Yayoi Kusama

The world had never seen anything like these colourful creations until Yayoi burst onto the scene.

Known as the 'princess of polka dots', Yayoi was inspired to cover everything in spots by visions she saw as a child (called 'hallucinations').

Although she makes different kinds of art – paintings, sculptures, large installations – they are all covered in her trademark polka dots.

Being a young, female Japanese artist, Yayoi had to overcome many obstacles to become one of the world's most successful creators. Her mental health has not always been good, but she's never stopped making art.

As well her artistic career, Yayoi has worked as an author, filmmaker and designer. She has referred to her work as "art medicine", as expressing herself helps her to feel better.

Learn more about Yayoi as you explore her colourful studio on the next page.

As a child, Yayoi had a hallucination that spotty **flowers** were talking to her, which has influenced her work throughout her whole life.

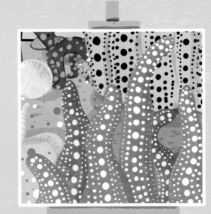

Yayoi made some giant inflatable sculptures so people could wander around them and **immerse** themselves in her world.

Yayoi has created lots of **pumpkin** sculptures. She says that pumpkins help her to feel safe and to overcome her fears.

She has created famous '**infinity rooms**', made of lots of little lights inside a room of mirrors, giving the effect that the dots of light go on forever.

Things to spot

Six small, arty **mice**

A pink **paintbrush pot**

Some spilt **black paint**

A **birthday cake**

A green and blue **spotty dog**

Answers

Did you find everything?
Check your answers below.

p8–9: Leonardo da Vinci

p12–13: Claude Monet

p16–17: Vincent van Gogh

p20–21: Henri Matisse

p24–25: Pablo Picasso

p28–29: Salvador Dalí

p32–33: Frida Kahlo

p36–37: Andy Warhol

p40–41: Yayoi Kusama

Test your knowledge

1. This lover of bold colours had an unusual pet called Bonito.

2. Don't be a square! You could never feel blue in this artist's mixed-up studio.

3. Join this artist for their last supper and they might treat you to a musical interlude.

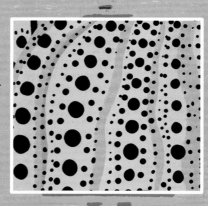

4. You'd better be dressed in your best polka dots if you visit this wild and wonderful studio.

5. You'll probably find this artist painting a sunny self-portrait.

6. This eccentric artist stands out in a crowd with their elaborate moustache.

7. This artist makes a great 'impression' with their amazing garden.

8. Stop to smell the flowers but make sure this artist doesn't 'leaf' you behind in their sunny studio!

9. This fun-loving artist is as POPular now as he was in the 1960s.

1. Frida Kahlo
2. Pablo Picasso
3. Leonardo da Vinci
4. Yayoi Kusama
5. Vincent van Gogh
6. Salvador Dalí
7. Claude Monet
8. Henri Matisse
9. Andy Warhol

Art Movements

Renaissance Art
Over 500 years ago, artists such as Leonardo da Vinci drew detailed human anatomy and used new techniques like perspective to create lifelike artwork.

Impressionism
Impressionists were all about capturing the 'impression' of something at the moment they saw it.

Post-Impressionism
This art style aimed to capture feelings rather than create something lifelike.

Surrealism
Artists combined the real and the imaginary to create strange, dreamlike work.

Expressionism
Artists painted their emotions and feelings using bold colours and unusual shapes.

Cubism
Artists used geometric shapes to show different angles at the same time.

Fauvism
Artists used bright colours, simple shapes and rough brushstrokes.

Pop Art
Artists used images from everyday life, like movie posters and advertisments, to create playful art.

Conceptual Art
The idea behind the artwork is more important than how it looks, and artists use many different mediums.